MOMMYTRACKED

Mommy Tracked

HOW TO TAKE AUTHENTIC
RISKS & FIND SUCCESS ON
YOUR TERMS

Sohee Jun, Ph.D.

LIONCREST

PUBLISHING

MOMMYTRACKED

How to Take Authentic Risks and Find Success On Your Terms

ISBN   978-1-5445-0834-4 *Hardcover*

978-1-5445-0832-0 *Paperback*

978-1-5445-0833-7 *Ebook*

To my forever loves and the reason I do
anything: Tyler, Emma, and Noah.

Contents

———

Introduction

————

Do you ever feel like you're on a path that's not your own? That you've lost touch of some of the pieces that made you whole? That at the end of the day, you're spent because you've given so much of yourself to the "shoulds" of work and family? That you're burning the candle at both ends, as a mother and an ambitious professional, but that you're not able to give enough of yourself to either? That you can't shake the sense that there's a more fulfilling path than the one you're currently on? Do you feel depleted? In constant guilt?

I get it, and I've been there.

For a large portion of my career, I worked in corporate America, and I felt like I brushed up against a rigid set of parameters that didn't feel right for me. When I became a mom, the rigid parameters felt even more stifling. I felt like I got put on the "mommytrack," a slowing of the big projects, the highly visible roles, etc., in anticipation of family needs. But did I want that? What did the *right* mommytrack look like for me? I wanted to find a way to live a life that felt fully integrated—but I wasn't sure how. I seemed to be chasing the solution to a problem that, for a long time, I couldn't concretely identify and name.

Early in my career, I didn't know what to ask for (or that I had permission to ask it). I wasn't used to flexing my risk-taking muscle. At that point in my life, I had taken very few big risks—you know the type of risks I'm talking about. The kind of risk that feels so scary, yet you know you need to do? What I *did* know was that the traditional way people approached careers in corporate America didn't feel authentic to me, yet I still had a strong ambitious bone. I got my Ph.D., and at the time, I thought I wanted to climb the traditional ladder and make it to the top. All the way to the top. Before I had children, I thought I should want that promotion or that big project that would provide the visibility to upper execs. I felt like I deserved it, yet I was oftentimes at odds with myself. I faced a lot of tension at the difference between the life I thought I could carve out and the one I was living, causing internal struggles and guilt.

So. Much. Guilt!

After having not one, but three beautiful kids, I felt it all the time. Sometimes, I thought I wasn't home enough, like

I was missing out on too much when my kids were little. All of their firsts, the crawling, the walking, the first foods, you get the picture. Then, other times I felt like I wasn't fully leaning into work, not taking on those high profile projects, not staying as late as everyone else—or, if I did, feeling guilty about the fact that I was missing bath time and/or bedtime. I was in a swirl of guilt. I was trying so hard to overcompensate in both roles, and it left me depleted all the time. It was lose-lose and I was on a fast, inauthentic track to burnout.

Through lots of reflection, pivotal experiences, and personal introspection, the voice inside of me said that what I really wanted and desperately needed was an integrated life. To pursue a path that was in alignment with my values and priorities for the phase and season of life I was in. To feel fulfilled and to be free from the confines of a traditional path or life and to be living one that was wholly my own. Defined by me.

And I did it, eventually. Through hard-won lessons and lots of trial and error, I now feel like I'm firing on all cylinders. Today, I have the ability to identify and take risks that are important to me. I have the work life I had envisioned for so long. For me, that means owning my own consulting firm, working with top-notch clients who energize me—primarily ambitious women who have families and want a coach to get them to their "what's next." At the same time, I have the family life I envisioned, spending quality time with my partner and children and they are both fully interwoven. No more compartmentalization and guilt. However, this didn't happen overnight. After getting my Ph.D. in Organizational Psychology and now twenty years in the field, I've had the pleasure of having worked with world-renowned Fortune 500 companies in media and entertainment as well as high-tech companies, startups, financial-services providers, and engineering firms. I've also had the good fortune to coach over fifty leaders and high performing women during this time. This book is a culmination of those experiences and my own that have gotten me here.

I'm in a flow state, and I feel much more integrated than I've ever been in my life.

The risks I took and the path I walked—and am still walking today, I might add—might not feel true for you. Your path *will* look different, as will the seasons of your life. That's all okay. If there's anything I want to bring awareness to in this book, it's that you don't have to follow a formula for success because *you* get to define it. *You* get to choose what success looks like in your life.

Re-read that last part as many times as it takes for it to sink in, and then say it louder for your ambitious girlfriends. Are you ready?

WHAT TO EXPECT

You may feel like you're on the mommytrack, but what they don't tell you is that at the end of the track isn't some standard destination. You're laying those tracks, move by move and risk by risk. Right now and tomorrow. You decide where you will end up—and then, where you'll go next.

In this book, we're going to unpack that idea and so many more. You'll learn why approaches like "finding balance" and "doing it all" are traps, especially if you tend toward the perfectionism side of the spectrum. (I'll raise my hand there!)

I'll show you how to identify your values and priorities, rethink risk and fear and the roles they play in your life, and internalize (once and for all) that it is impossible to move forward without self-care. I'll share how you can grant yourself grace in making authentic choices in varying seasons of your life, and together we'll discuss how you can take that first micro action—and the one after that, and that—to move you forward.

In this book, you'll find steps you can take, whether big or small, to live a life that feels integrated—and, more importantly, authentic to you. I'll share easy, actionable tools, reflection questions, and strategies you can implement to help get you unstuck. And, don't worry, the "Pause Points" within the chapters are meant as questions for you to think about. The reflection questions at the end of each chapter are meatier and much more thought-provoking. They will require a bit more time on your part, so be sure to jot down your thoughts. And while answering these may take more minutes—it's so worth it, I promise!

I'll also share more of my own journey along the way to show you what's possible, including both the wins and the challenges. I'm putting myself out there in this book because I have walked this path. In fact, I am *still* walking this path. Is it hard? Yes. Does it get easier with every step I take? That's a yes, too. I'm never done because I'm continuously evolving, just like you.

That said, if you're looking for a book that gives you a predefined, rigid process to follow to help you attain someone else's version of success, this isn't that book. Just put it down. If you're looking for a book to share only the positive side of risk-taking and sugarcoat how challenging or scary it can be, this isn't that book either.

I'm showing up here, wholly. If you do, too, what I know for sure is that the strategies in this book will help you form a plan that feels true for you. It will help you move through the next day, the next week, the next year. It will clearly help you forge your own path, *chosen* mommytrack by *chosen* mommytrack, toward an integrated life. But you have to do the work, too, because this isn't a passive read.

Stay open to the journey because you 100 percent deserve a fully integrated life you love!

You picked up this book for a reason. If you're feeling boxed in, I am here to nudge you unstuck. I want you to feel like you have your own coach in your pocket, here when you need me.

Here's that first nudge. Let's get started.

CHAPTER ONE

Debunking the "Mommy Balance" Myth

———

"You can have it all. Just not all at once."

—OPRAH WINFREY

We all want the "mommy hack," right? The secret to doing it all? To finding that elusive "balance" or "work-life integration" we think everyone else has? I mean, it's all we as women ever talk about. It's mentioned at every conference, every interview done with successful women, or on panels with women speakers. The first question out of the gate of every interview with a kick-ass, successful woman is, "How do you do it all?" For me, I would feel myself cringe because it's perpetuating the myth that you can do all the things without missing a beat, on your own. Every time that question is asked, it reinforces that this elusive goal is attainable... if only you just tried harder. It makes us question why we're not doing enough, being enough, saying enough, whatever enough that we don't have all the plates spinning, in perfect rotation, all the time. No plates dropped.

Oh, by the way, a hack like that doesn't exist. You can't crack this mommy balance perfection! What I've learned through hard-won risks, some falls and lots of getting back up, is that the key is to build a life that's in line with your values and priorities, that is also representative of the season that you're in, and that doesn't need cracking in the first place.

That's not easy to do, but it *is* very possible. Intrigued? We'll discuss how in the pages of this book.

Still, for the skeptics, as an ambitious woman, you may be thinking you can be the exception, the one to do it all, the anomaly. I see you so clearly because guess what? I *was* you. I was you to a point that I once fell asleep on my couch, in the middle of the day, surrounded by my three children. They were seven, five, and two at the time, and I clearly remember that I was "to the bones" tired. Ever felt that level of exhaustion? My guess is that many of you can relate to this. That was me, and on that particular day, I ran out of gas. Fell hard asleep, sitting upright, as my kids watched. They needed me, but still, there I was: out cold.

To be fair, as you may have imagined and probably relate to, it had been a long day. In addition to the fifty-plus hour workweeks I was taking on—complete with back-to-back meetings, lots of deliverables, and a boss with high expectations—I'd also volunteered to coach my five-year-old's soccer team. That meant more activities on my calendar that had run out of free hours. More meetings, more planning time, more certifications, and more everything!

Still, both my partner and I wanted to encourage our daughter's love of sports, and of course it seemed doable in my ambitious, "do it all" frame of mind. I signed up willingly without thinking about how the decision would impact my already tanked energy level. We participated in and coached sports activities for our other children, right? It all had to be equal. No question. Like many women, how depleted I already felt didn't even come into play; I wanted to please everyone, be a "great" mom, a high performer at work and make sure I delivered in all areas of my life. Full stop.

It's important to note that I didn't just want to coach; I wanted to coach her team *well*. You can see where this story is going. I put tons of unknowing pressure on myself to perform at a high level, to be the best coach possible for her, and to ensure the team was having fun while learning key skills! The stress even boiled over into my marriage. The day I got to a point where I literally couldn't keep my eyes open, I found myself frantically and stressfully asking my partner for tips on what to do for the first session with the kids, because I had nothing prepared—again, for a five-year-old's soccer practice.

That particular Saturday, we'd gone to soccer in the morning. It was also grocery shopping day. And did I mention I was already running on empty?

I shuffled in the house post-soccer and post-grocery store, three kids and bags in tow. Finally, I reached a relieving point in what felt like (and likely was) *days:* we legitimately had ten minutes of quiet time. We all sat on the couch. The kids were really looking forward to some non-rushed Mommy time, but I immediately fell asleep fast. In fact, I've never fallen so heavily asleep, so quickly. I don't even remember how it happened, exactly—that's how quickly I was out. What I do remember, though, is it set me on the path to learning that there is such a thing as too much. That I need to make some hard choices. That burnout is unhealthy, even if it looks like progress.

This knowledge didn't happen overnight. I had years of conditioning to undo—starting with revisiting my answer to one question that had been a major theme in my life up to that point.

"HOW DO YOU DO IT ALL?"

The Pew Research Center says that moms spend more time with their kids today than they did in the sixties.

Oh, and they also spend more time at work.

So, how does that add up?

Hint: it doesn't, but we can trick ourselves into thinking it does, at least for a time. When I was leading a team at a large entertainment company, I had many women come up to me and ask "how I did it." I took those conversations as opportunities to be honest with them. They saw a smart, ambitious, put-together woman, working and leading a team, on the up n' up, with three small children. I shed light into the inner workings, telling them I had to have a lot of help at home to keep everything above water. In fact, I even shared that had I not had my mom to help me and had my partner not had a flexible schedule, I wouldn't have had a third child—that's how seriously I valued support and knew I needed it to make my life run. My life may have appeared seamless to them on the outside, but there was significant thought, planning, calendaring, and movements behind the scenes with lots of helping hands. My hope in sharing this truth with these women was that they would understand that I wasn't doing it all. That if it looks like someone is "doing it all,"...it wasn't without a significant amount of support from their tribe. I know for me, I leaned heavily on mine so that I could succeed at work.

Still, even though my conversations with these women were rooted in honesty—and they truly were—I'd be lying if I said their questions alone didn't give me superficial surges of confidence. I got reinforcement from their questions, even while giving authentic and genuine responses. Others recognizing my success at "doing it all" amplified my perfectionist tendencies.

Yes, I'd think, somewhere in my psyche. See, I'm making it work and I'm serving as a role model for other women! I need to keep it going.

This external indicator of what I *thought* was success fed my ego, and it was counterproductive. I wanted to do more, as a result. I had to keep the persona up. It was more than just a desire; it was a responsibility—which, to a recovering perfectionist, is nonnegotiable. Now I had another group of people I couldn't let down—the moms in the office who needed someone to look up to. I had to be a different kind of role model—one who was the leader, who managed her team, who delivered on big projects, who was healthy and up on the latest trends, who was an attentive mom, who made time for her partner...the list goes on and on.

It's an exhausting sentence to write, but trust me, it was even more exhausting to live and sustain.

We've all replayed the "doing it all" tape in our minds at

one point or another, probably without thinking what that means. Consider for a moment: How many women are living like I was, in quiet desperation and trapped trying to juggle everything? Is that you? How many women are following the wrong script for their lives?

In my corporate America days, the term "mommytracked" was thrown around for women who either wanted or had kids and it put them on a less desirable/less challenging path based on assumptions that we wanted to take a back seat. In this book, we'll redefine that term so that it means we take ownership of our whole lives and actively work to define our fully integrated lives on our own terms.

Part of that is rejecting how we are conditioned by a society that shows us this nebulous goal of "balance" as the carrot dangling in front of motherhood. The problem, though, is that the finish line keeps moving. We never reach it, but we judge ourselves against this moving target all the same.

More than that, we judge each other and do the compare game.

Because the mommy world is so confusing and can be hard to navigate, especially for first-time moms, we make judgments and try to make sense of how we fit within it—and how others do, too. This isn't necessarily conscious; it's just how our brain works. We short-circuit to that preprogramming. If we see someone who has a career, kids, and still seems put together, we make assumptions that these women must know something we don't, or they have help, or both. If we see someone who has a career, kids, and seems (to us) falling apart at the seams, we make assumptions then, too. Many times, stereotypes can creep into our minds unknowingly.

You left your kids in after-school care? I would never do that.

You didn't make it to the class party because you had a meeting? What are your priorities?

You left your job to stay home with your baby for six months? What about all the ground you'll lose in your career?

These stereotypes only feed the narrative society tells us about ourselves, and we need to actively work to squash it. That's hard and even harder to do in the age of social media, especially when social media feeds this impulse with the picture of the beautifully clean, happy baby and the glowing mom, perfectly happy. You know the pictures I'm talking about. I've probably posted many of those images myself. Whether consciously or unconsciously, most of us have played into this "perfect" vision of motherhood, whiting out the real parts and only showing the squeaky clean version. This adds to the myth of balance, and it damages those that aspire to that level of unattainable perfection.

We all judge each other, walking around with a picture of how things "should" look. Each time that doesn't match up, we make a story in our heads about ourselves and about other mothers. It's only when we can honestly connect and have conversations about the truths of being a mom that we can start to have compassion for ourselves and others.

But before we can get to that point, we must actively avoid one of the biggest traps ambitious women face: perfectionism.

THE PERFECTIONIST TRAP

Okay, I'll admit that being a perfectionist was such a part of my DNA that sometimes I didn't even realize I was acting from that mindset at all. And the word "perfectionist" gets a bad rap, and there's a lot of baggage around it. When I hear it, I think, *whoa, that's not me.* To me, it's simply always been my nature to go full throttle at home and at work and to control how things happen as much as I can. Perfectionist, anyone?

I'm not alone; from my over twenty years of coaching highly ambitious women, I've found this creeps up subconsciously for lots of us, too. While common, it can manifest differently, and it comes from different formative experiences.

For me, my experience with the perfectionist trap has a

lot to do with how I was rewarded growing up. In a South Korean immigrant family that didn't show much affection or talk about emotions or things of substance, I was the youngest of two girls. My sister and I were opposites in many ways; she got attention for being loud and sometimes very dramatic. Given that, I found a way to get attention by being the "good" girl. For being quiet and having little perceived needs. For getting good grades, for taking care of myself as best as I could—even if I didn't know how. For being dutiful in a lot of ways that, culturally, were expected of me.

In other words, in order to shine and get noticed in my own family, I had to be mature beyond my years and handle my shit.

From a very young age, that became not just a part of my personality, but a baseline for how I moved through the world. This programming stayed with me throughout my early years and into college, where I felt I not only had to have great grades but also a huge social circle and all the extracurriculars to go with it. I appeared to have it all together externally while the reality was, I struggled to have it all contained. Many times I was falling apart on the inside.

I specifically recall once, in my early twenties, my partner and I flew to Hawaii for a weekend wedding. In beautiful Hawaii! The following week, I was responsible for putting on a large leadership development program that would span several days. What would you guess I was doing all weekend? YUP! You probably guessed it! I was preparing and rehearsing and going through all the details over and again. To make sure I had it all "right," I missed most of the celebratory event besides the wedding itself! Seriously. I remember my mother-in-law commenting that I was such a hard worker and so committed. And that reinforcement came from a good place, but it just fed my over rehearsing "control" tendencies even more. Looking back, I know the leadership program would have been just as good had I not over-prepared. In fact, I know that it would have even been better, as I'd have been more likely to show up as my true self. And, let's not even talk about the amazing people and events I missed over the course of that weekend.

The perfectionist trap was (and is) real, and I've been tangled all up in it.

Even today, I think it's hard to let go of entirely. I've gotten much better, and I'm very intentional about not falling into my old habit of gathering my confidence from reinforcement of those perfectionist tendencies. Still, I grapple with it from time to time, and I have to be really honest with myself about how I integrate my life and what takes priority based on my context and values. There's a lot of behind-the-scenes thinking, reflecting, and checking in with myself to make sure that perfectionism isn't leading me, but the result is so worth it!

If you're reading this and thinking, I get this to a degree, and I'm a bit of a perfectionist myself. So what?

Here's what: when you get so into the nitty-gritty of the little things in your everyday life and try to make everything perfect, it stops you from moving forward and keeps you in the weeds. It not only strips away the organic moments and the joy of "just being" and being authentic in that moment, but it makes you overanalyze and get into control mode. For example, in my many years in corporate America, I've seen high performing, amazing, talented women obsess over their emails before sending them, wanting to word them *just the right way.* They ruminate over how it will be received, how the tone may be taken, and the exact wording of things. It's practical and even advisable to want your communication to convey your message well, but it's not practical or advisable to rewrite the whole thing three times because it's *just not right* yet. This is also detrimental to your goal of showing up authentically at work. Plus, in today's fast-paced world, we can't afford to linger too long on perfecting a message. I once worked with a woman who had this exact issue, overanalyzing everything instead of simply sending her thoughts. It not only hindered her day-to-day work life, but it also hindered her overall experience of work because she couldn't be herself. She was always guarded, even in email communications.

This issue goes all the way to the top. When I was climbing

the ranks at a financial services company in my twenties, I had two female managers who were smart and extremely talented in their own ways. They would literally read my emails word-for-word and had me change things so they were "perfect," according to their view. This wasn't because they were bad people—they were just so deep in their own ingrained perfectionist trap, perhaps brought on by the added weight of gender conditioning and being females in leadership positions, that they tried to adjust how others communicated. This was ineffective, as they were in the weeds and spending time reading emails instead of being strategic and broad thinking for the company.

I've also seen high performing women habitually over pre-pare, much like I did when I should have been enjoying the beach wedding festivities in Hawaii all those years ago. This is another common example in corporate life: you over-rehearse for a presentation, pitch, or anything that involves you talking to a group of people. How this shows up in my coaching with women is couched as needing more "exec-utive presence."

Note that I'm not saying don't prepare. I'm saying don't overdo. There comes a point in which our efforts don't add to the outcome. We try to orchestrate everything we do and say, even down to inflection, to sound credible and have charisma. That all leads to a lack of authenticity and a lot of time wasted. This is a great example of how we try to be perfect but see it disguised as productivity. That's why perfectionism is such a sneaky thing! There is a difference between preparing and trying to control. Let's let that one marinate.

In the book, *How Women Rise*, Sally Helgesen notes that striving to be perfect creates stress for not just the individual but for those around that individual. Why? Because it's based on expectations that human beings may occasionally live up to but which cannot be sustained over time. Not only that, striving to be perfect creates a negative mindset in which you're bothered by every little thing that goes wrong, since even a small mistake can "ruin" the whole. And it keeps you riveted on details, distracting you from the big picture.

LEVELING THE PLAYING FIELD

One way to combat perfectionism—which, again, is fuel on the fire of that unhealthy balance myth—is to start from the beginning. It's to understand how our gender identity played a role in how we got to this point. And it also helps to know that it isn't just "us" or who we are; there are definitely bigger societal forces at play here.

In Reshma Saujani's book *Brave Not Perfect: Fear Less, Fail More, and Live Bolder*—she discusses how little girls are simply conditioned and socialized very differently than little boys. It isn't even intentional or conscious, but it's so deeply programmed and can be subtle.

Of appearance, we tell boys, "Sure, it's a little muddy. It's okay."

Of appearance, we tell girls, "Don't get too messy, sweetie. We just fixed your hair!"

Of risk, we tell boys, "Go play!"

Of risk, we tell girls, "Sit here next to mommy. You're a good girl. Be nice."

And so on. You get the picture.

These socialization differences not only happen socially with friends and family but it's also alive and well in the school system. From the get-go, boys are encouraged to raise their hands more. Specifically, as kids enter fourth and fifth grade, the attitude and confidence demarcation becomes even more evident. Around this time, studies show that girls start deferring to boys. They may start to opt-out of science and math-related activities. They start to get rewarded differently not just at home, but by what they know of the world.

These socializations take many different forms and come

from parents, teachers, authority figures, and society. It's also in the marketing of everything, movies, books, and the list goes on and on. Girls have a different experience in this world than boys, and it starts from the beginning. Simple as that and important to be aware of what we're all working with.

Many of these comments come from people who are well-intentioned yet simply unaware of how the bias inherent in their language matters in shaping our daily behaviors, and ultimately, many of our struggles as adults. And again, here's why this matters: the result is that many of us grew up knowing we needed to be good! To be tame. To be steady. To be contained. To be put together and *play small!* To care what others think over what we want and to stop listening to our most important guide: our inner voice/gut.

In her book *Playing Big*, Tara Mohr shares that study after study has shown that girls spend more time preparing their schoolwork than boys. Even from a young age, preparation and even overpreparation is a stronger behavior pattern in girls than in boys! Studies also show that women will spend more time preparing for a task or test (or meetings or presentations) than men.

Let me ask you this: How many times have you stopped yourself from doing something you really wanted to do because you:

1. Cared more about what others thought of that action/thought
2. Knew they wouldn't "approve" or agree with you
3. Felt it was "too risky" or too "out there"

...All this despite the fact that your inner voice was informing you that it would be the right thing for you?

This has hindered us as a gender because we, collectively, don't intuitively show up as our authentic selves until we know it's safe. And there's a lot that's not safe in the loss of control on the other side of perfectionism, isn't there?

What we internalize as little girls shows up for us as women in corporate life, for sure! It hinders us from feeling safe enough to show our authentic selves. It prevents us from moving faster up the ladder or being put on bigger and complex projects—if that feels true for us—because we spend our time overanalyzing **if** we're qualified, **if** we're ready, **if** we're the right person, **if** we're prepared enough, **if** we can handle it and to ultimately value the opinions and thoughts of others versus our own inner knowing. The vast majority of my female coaching clients grapple with many or all of these thoughts and it feels so real in our heads.

Don't get me wrong, I know I felt this way too. I spent so much of my early life grinding everything out. That's a word I hear a lot, especially from women. It's similar to the notion of keeping your "nose to the grindstone," which—even in verbiage alone—applies some level of discomfort is necessary to achieve. The assumption that we grind to perfection, and that there's merit in that grind, is (for most of us) baked-in to our gender experience. The important distinction is to know that qualifications and experience are, of course, necessary in work and life. However, many of the women I've coached or worked with overdo it and wait too long.

I'm not doing any of that in my house.

I have two boys and a girl, and I'm trying to level the playing field as much as I can. I'm very conscious and intentional about how I raise my daughter, careful not to reward her verbally or otherwise based on what she wears or how contained and quiet she is or on how she looks. Today, she's an eight-year-old badass ice hockey player, who is opinionated, carefree, sure of herself, and blossoming every day—and I love that! On the other side of the coin, I am careful to raise my boys as their whole selves, too! Not muting their emotions and what makes them unique and encouraging them to feel all of their feelings and normalizing it for them. I often ask all my children equalizing questions like "What is going on for you?" "How are you feeling?" and "What does that feel like?" In my family, it's more important that we help grow their emotional aptitude and emotional intelligence, which includes being self-aware, than anything else.

Isn't it time to drop that heavy load of perfectionism?

INTEGRATION VERSUS BALANCE

At this point, we understand the link between perfectionism and our quest for "mommy balance." We also understand that the only thing in that sentence that is actually real is perfectionism. The hacks? The squeaky-clean-all-the-time mommy balance? Forget them.

Well...kind of.

True balance *is* possible—that is, if you ditch your idea of perfection and understand that you can redefine what balance means to you during different seasons and phases of your unique life. A better word for this—and one I encourage you to internalize—is integration. I firmly believe that you can have it all, but not all at once. Let's let that one sit for a moment. This is also where integration comes in. We've been so conditioned to believe in some externally defined notion of having it all, all at the same time, and to keep all of the balls in the air, never to be dropped.

Balance feels antiquated. Unachievable. Integration, on the other hand, means you are actively working to make space for what's important to you based on your values and priorities. This principle is backed by research, and women are making the paradigm switch. I know because

I've coached many of them. Can we pause for a second and reflect on these two words: "Balance" and "Integration?" What comes to mind when you think of the first and then the second?

Take a woman we'll call Mary, for example. Mary is a former colleague of mine with two children under five years old and a job at a corporate company. At one time—when she had only one child and more time to devote to her role—the demanding position worked for her. After she had her second child, though, she felt misaligned. She wanted more of an integration between her work and home life, so she got curious. She wanted to take the risk of staying home directly after her youngest child was born, so—with the support of her partner—she did. Later, she realized staying home wasn't in line with her values, so she decided the next milestone for her was returning to that corporate track.

Because she'd already exercised that risk muscle when she made the choice to leave, the choice to return was an easier one to make. Not only that, but she returned on *her* terms, setting clear boundaries with the team bringing her back on board. For example, she told them she was *really* going to leave at 5 p.m. She told them she was *really* going to be "off" when she wasn't in the office, not responding to emails, etc. This setup allowed her to be more integrated with both work and family. She's still within that context, and it's still working for her.

But guess what? When it doesn't work anymore, she'll make a new context. That's what integration is: iterative, not binary, and based on your priorities and values for the season you're in. Repeat this sentence.

ENGAGE WITH THE WORD "SEASONS"

Mary and countless other clients have found work-life integration partly because they've been able to engage with and embrace the word *seasons*. For our purposes, seasons are defined by milestones or pivotal moments within the larger context of your life. Did you just get married? Divorced? Are you planning to have children? Are you working for a promotion? Our experiences in this life are unique, but change is universal. Examining these changes as markers will naturally help you define a season of your life. For example, I stayed home with my first child until he was eight months old. I distinctly recall deciding that when he hit the one-year mark, things would look different for me; I knew I would rejoin the corporate side of the workforce. His growth was a signal for *my* growth. It was the changing of a season.

Sometimes, as women, we can often feel innately that our lives are shifting—or that we want to take steps to shift them ourselves. Sometimes, though, everything is not so obvious. Sometimes we may feel discontent about our situation and not know why; this is often a signal of a change in seasons (or a need for one). In these cases, it helps to take a step back and determine how fulfilled we are in the areas that matter most to us. (*Note:* If you struggle with this notion, refer to the Fulfillment Scale at the end of this chapter for help.) To do this, you must be willing to take an intentional pause so that you can look inward.

TRUST YOURSELF

How long has it been since you turned inward, into yourself, into that small but persistent voice inside of you for guidance? For me, it took years to tune into my inner wisdom and then many more years to trust it enough to take action. If you weren't controlling or anticipating your reaction(s), how would you show up in this moment? With friends? With colleagues? With your family?

Reaching work-life integration means trusting yourself enough to show up authentically—even if that means failing now and then. It's about understanding that you can be present in situations life throws at you and simply let yourself be. It's about trusting your responses and abilities without overanalyzing everything to pieces and doing retrospective "shoulds." It's about having peace around how you show up in the world, a comfort in knowing that you can handle things now or pause and come back to them later—and that both are okay.

If this sounds impossible, it's not. Let's take another step back.

Ask yourself: When you are comfortable and relaxed, what does that look like for you? How does that feel? Maybe you don't have an answer right now. Maybe you're too tightly wound in the grip of perfectionism that the question itself stresses you out. That's okay. Come back to it. Remember, I'm the coach in your pocket. I'm not going anywhere.

Trusting yourself isn't just helpful to you as a person; it can be helpful to those around you, too. Personally, it has greatly impacted my career. The more comfortable I became with myself, the more I focused on other people. Those other people were then able to feel a genuineness and authenticity from me that helped us connect—which, in the end, is what we all want.

Today, the bulk of my coaching is around helping women be more authentic in their choices and more effective in dealing with others—handling conflict, communicating better, and so on. Regardless of the industry—from entertainment to finance—human interaction is the common thread. In the corporate world and now as a coach, I've found that when I stopped worrying about how I was showing up *to* others, I could focus more on how I showed up *for* others. I could focus more on how I can be of service instead of trying to control the outcome. And that means we all win.

If you have a voice inside of you that comes up every now and then and whispers about the life you want, or project you want to tackle, or experience you want to have, get curious with it. Explore what that looks like. Maybe even write it down for yourself. Trust that the voice inside is guiding you in the right direction.

REDEFINE "SUCCESS"

Now, here's the thing: striving for integration often means redefining what a successful life looks like for you.

We've been taught that success looks one way—and that way is very linear. When I was in my early thirties, I played that game. I was highly focused on climbing the traditional corporate ladder and racking up those promotions. I watched as my colleagues were moving up, getting promotions, and I equated those actions to success. Yet the more promotions I got, the bigger my scope and responsibilities became, the unhappier I felt. I felt trapped. I felt at times suffocated by a path that wasn't authentic to me. I felt depleted and starved for creativity, play, and freedom. It didn't occur to me to look at success in a more holistic way. I never thought of success as being able to do the things that give me joy and energy. Yet...

But now I do.

Did you ever notice that we ask children: "What do you want to be when you grow up?" Inherent in that question is that there's *one* destination, *one* peak to reach, *one* epitome of success and one path.

What if that's the wrong question? What if success isn't the rung at the top of a ladder? What if it's more of a jungle gym instead? What if it's a series of destinations? What if there are more ways to climb it than straight up?

I encourage you to choose what gives you energy and what fulfills you. This might feel scary and risky to do at first but give it a try. Then, do that. *That* is success, and whatever it looks like season to season is valid. When you start making decisions based on your inner compass, you show others that they can, too. And that's a win!

PAUSE POINT

Q: What does having it all look like for you?

Q: How has "mommy balance" played a role in your life?

Q: Reflecting back on your own life, can you identify the roots of your perfectionist tendencies?

Q: How has perfectionism stopped you from showing up authentically?

PAY AUTHENTICITY FORWARD

Maya Angelou said, "When you know better, you do better." By redefining success, you show everyone at the bottom of the ladder or the base of the jungle gym that there's another way. I wish someone had shown me that sooner. Instead, I worried I would look unambitious if I took a detour or chose a different path, and I did myself a disservice by ruminating on that each time I thought to make a change. I didn't want to disappoint others.

So, what I didn't tell you about the time I fell asleep on the couch surrounded by my kids: that before that, I was coming off a debilitating case of postpartum depression and charging headfirst into a new leadership role, my life packed with back-to-back meetings and huge responsibilities. There was no time to breathe. I didn't know that my body was signaling me to take a break—which it clearly was, as I'll explain more when we talk about self-care in chapter four.

What I did do around this time, however, was reach out to start a real conversation about burnout. I shared a post on Facebook that spoke a little to how I was feeling, and the response was overwhelming. So many women responded.

"Yes, this is hard."

"Oh my God, I have been there."

The responses helped me internalize Angelou's quote. I realized we don't have enough women showing each other that it's okay to make authentic choices, that it's okay to say when something doesn't feel good, that it's okay to be authentic about what isn't working, and to let down your guard. When we pay this authenticity forward, we can help others see that they can make different choices for themselves. When we act as nonjudgmental listeners and thought partners, we can lift each other up.

Reaching this point takes curiosity. When you start from this genuine place, you take away the defensiveness and posturing we may have about who we are and how our pride is tied to our definition of success. If we can sit with someone and simply say, "Tell me more," that curiosity will open doors. It will open us up to our human stories and help us let go of the bifurcation and the labels.

As adults, we tend to internalize observations and interactions in ways that help reinforce our biases, unconsciously. It's like our brain is a filing cabinet.

There's another stressed-out post from Susie. She clearly can't handle everything on her plate.

Today at school drop off, Erica looked pretty disheveled. She clearly wasn't taking care of herself.

There's Olivia, running the PTA again. I don't know how she does it. She must have it all figured out.

I've encountered judgment in the working mom circle, and I've encountered judgment in the stay-at-home circle. I've probably done some of the judging myself, too. I admit that. It's all counterproductive to women who are on the journey to living their most authentic lives.

At this time, women have more choices than ever before to make unique decisions about how they want to live their whole, best lives. The more we share our stories with courage and honesty, the more we can share that all paths are okay and should be celebrated! It's time we looked at our inner filing cabinets in the opposite way. Instead of reinforcing our beliefs, the stories that fill those folders provide context and opportunities for connection.

We teach our kids to be good listeners and good friends, right? What if we applied that same advice to ourselves, tuning into our inner voice about what feels right and true in this season of our lives...and gave ourselves kudos for that?

We're going to identify how fulfilled you feel in the biggest areas of your life. Rank your life on a scale of one to five, using the key below, in the following areas.

Fulfillment Scale

1	2	3	4	5
Extremely Unfulfilled	Unfulfilled	Neutral	Fulfilled	Extremely Fulfilled

Be honest with yourself. No one will judge you, and the gaps here are opportunities to reflect. Remember, there is no perfect score.

1. How fulfilled are you in your role as a mother? ....

2. How fulfilled are you in your role as a partner? ....

3. How fulfilled are you spiritually? ....

4. How fulfilled are you physically? ....

5. How fulfilled are you emotionally? ....

6. How fulfilled are you mentally? ....

7. How fulfilled are you in your career? ....

8. How fulfilled are you in your friendships? ....

Why did you choose the ratings you did? Take time to reflect on your responses. Which responses had 1s or 2s?

....

....

....

....

To work through the concepts in this chapter, and building on your answers in the Pause Points, ask yourself the following questions. Find yourself a quiet spot, grab your favorite beverage, and let's get going.

1. Who is your current career role model? Why? What messages either directly or indirectly are you receiving about success and having it all?

....

....

....

....

2. Looking back on your career and any female bosses you've had, how have they shaped who you are today?

....

....

....

....

3. What did you learn from the females in your life (your mom, siblings, bosses, etc.) about what you wanted to do or not do and how you wanted to live your life?

....

....

....

....

4. What is your current level of risk tolerance? Estimate if you need to, using the risk meter at the end of chapter three.

....

....

....

....

WHAT'S NEXT?

Perfection doesn't exist, and pretending it does merely contributes to the "mommy balance" myth and takes our energy away from what we need to be focusing on: work-life integration.

I guide and teach my clients to do their part in untangling this narrative, and I do the same work as well. For starters, take some time to reflect on the answers around the priority(ies) for you in this season of your life and how things would shift in your life based on those priorities. This will serve as your blueprint for the next chapters to come.

In the next chapter, we'll continue our Mommytracked journey. An important part of taking authentic risks and finding success on your terms is understanding what values and priorities you are basing those changes *on*. That way, you'll find a much more fluid integration of what you are passionate about as well as what (and who) brings you joy.

CHAPTER TWO

Identifying Your Values and Priorities

———

"Success is a lousy teacher."

—UNKNOWN

Before I had kids, I recall a moment when my girlfriend, who was married with a kid, and I were shopping and got onto some big questions about life. What was her experience with marriage? Why did she decide to have only one child? What was it like to be a parent? Would she do anything differently or not?

At the time, I wasn't even thinking of having children, but I was still curious. I remember telling her that if we did decide to have kids, I wanted to be involved, present, and there for their milestones, big and small. It wasn't crystal clear to me, on that day, what that would look like for me and my partner in actuality, but I had a definite knowing that I wanted to be actively involved.

I was simply having a conversation, but what I was also doing in that moment was innately talking about what I wanted for that season of my life—something that has remained true and anchored my decisions, even to this day. I was defining a value.

I believe this value was born of my experience as a latch-key kid. Growing up, my parents weren't there much—not because they didn't want to be, but because they were always working to make a better life for us. My story is similar to that of the many immigrants who chose to come to the States to make a new life. My parents often worked two or three jobs to make ends meet, so from a very young age, we needed to take care of ourselves and each other. My sister and I were told that we had to be there for each other; there were a lot of "shoulds" in my youth tied to family and expectations around it. It was hammered into me. Both of those experiences, one in which my parents couldn't be around, defined what I wanted, should I become a parent. That's a value that's deep-seated within me.

Besides family, other values of mine include wellness (emotional and physical), freedom, ambition, new experiences, curiosity, authenticity, and relationships. I have a whole list, and my priorities flow from there. Just to be clear, these values haven't always been the same. Yours may shift, too. As you grow and evolve, some values may stay consistent, but some may come off or on your list. That's normal and expected. It's the process of growing and with each new experience in life, your list will evolve accordingly.

Fast-forward to years after that shopping conversation. I had kids. I had a career. I still had my values, but I was in a showdown with priorities. I was feeling out of alignment because I was spending so much of my time at work, feeling less and less integrated, and always being so tired. While at times the work was exciting, I felt more and more that it took me away from my priorities of sharing more moments with my kids, and I wasn't sure what to do. My role and duties had changed, as it happens when you advance in a company. I found myself moving away from what I loved about my prior positions—the collaboration, creative problem solving with others, working directly with clients and having a direct impact—and more toward what sucked my energy, like the politics of being a leader and managing up. I was eager to expand on my experience of leading a team and being a guide and coach, but I also felt increasingly isolated and drained.

I asked around for advice from other women who were in leadership roles. After some thought, I even got creative, took a risk and proposed a different role. A role that would expand my skills in a different way, get my creative juices flowing again and allow me to step off the draining path I was on. When I felt like I was at my wit's end and talked about potentially leaving, my company countered my proposal and discussed the possibility of yet a different role—one with a promotion and with it, *more* responsibility. While a promotion is always enticing to a recovering perfectionist, nothing any of us came up with fit.

During this time, I was actively talking to my partner about what to do next. In our discussion, I talked about what I wanted most...the freedom to create my own schedule, be my own boss again, and really be more integrated into my kids' lives. Yet, the thought of doing this and taking the leap stressed me so much that I would sweat just thinking about it! Really. There were moments where I'd wake up at night with everything inside of me screaming to leave my job because it felt so binding and inauthentic to my values. Then, all the shoulds would come crying at me. I had this wonderful role, a coveted title, and I was paid well. I had the corner office with a great team of people who looked to me for guidance. I felt like I *should* be happy, but I was miserable—which added another layer of inner blaming. I wondered what was wrong with me. Who in her right mind would leave all this—and for what? To be an entrepreneur? To take a giant risk that might not pay off? What was I thinking? This type of circular thinking went on for a good long while. Yet when I dug really deep and got even more real, the truth is that at the end of this was another layer of fear. I didn't want to disappoint people. It's as simple and as complicated as that. The people who looked up to me, those who asked me back to the company to lead the team and gave me another opportunity, the team itself, my family, my mom...the list goes on and on.

And yet...

I could not escape the fact that it just *did not feel right*.

I'm not alone...many of the women I coach and have talked to feel a terrifying level of fear when they dig deep and think about living a life that's aligned with their values and priorities.

TIME TO GET CURIOUS

It all turned around for me when I allowed myself to get curious. I knew what *didn't* feel right, but what *would* feel right? And how far away was I from that endgame?

I started to ask myself more and more questions. I realized I liked the people I worked with and the team and the scope of the work, but other pieces were missing: I needed more freedom, the ability to command my own hours, and the space to work on projects with clients that truly fueled me. Most of all, I needed to not ask for permission to be where I needed to be...with my kids at their school, at their activities, or with clients.

As I answered these questions, it became increasingly easier for me to say that I needed to take the next step; for me, that meant returning to the consulting world. I even got as detailed as to write out what a "day in the life" would look like in this new season. Once I got the clarity, I knew the micro steps I needed to take to get there. So I took a risk in alignment with my values and priorities: I left and did just that.

Trust me, it wasn't easy! But it does show how our needs change from season to season. I went back to my company after having my first baby because I wanted that stability. I stayed there until it was no longer serving me. The company didn't change that much in that time; *I* did—my needs, my circumstances, my priorities. I used the power of getting curious as the portal to my discovery and growth. It wasn't the first time, and it won't be the last.

By the way, getting curious doesn't always need to lead to monumental change, like it did in my case. It's a tool anyone can use—and sometimes, it helps to ask out loud. Here's a great example: once I was walking to lunch with a colleague of mine, who works in finance. We hadn't caught up in a while, so I asked how everything was going in her life and work.

"I'm doing great!" she said. "But I've been thinking about what to do with my career. Right now, it seems there are really two choices for me. I can either go back and get my CPA officially and advance in the route I'm currently on. Or, *(and I can see her get more excited and heard her tone change as she said this)* I can look more into this coaching stuff that I've been doing on the side. I really love it."

I couldn't help but smile. "You're asking *me* what you should do next?" I said, stopping in my tracks. "You said yourself that you can continue the same path you are on now and take a test for something that you don't even seem interested in. Or, you could pursue this route that lights you up as you talk about it. I can see your energy around it. To me, it's pretty clear what you should do."

And she did—in a way that worked for her! She couldn't leave her job entirely because she was the primary breadwinner and was also putting a young child through school. So, for her, what felt like the right mix was to pick up more coaching clients on the side, to write more blogs on topics that she was passionate about and to get certified in coaching. Even though it was more work, she didn't feel depleted, because she was choosing tasks that *gave* her energy, not draining it. When I saw her again, months later, I could tell that she found the right mix for this season of her life and she was owning it!

This story is proof that your values and priorities can be extrapolated upon outside your day job—or, even within it.

I once coached a client, a lawyer who told me she was happiest when she was creating, especially writing. Creativity was a value for her and in truth, she wasn't looking for a dramatic job shift or life change. She simply wanted to discover if it was possible to be more fulfilled where she was.

I helped her get curious by asking: What does it look like to flex your creative muscles? Is it possible to do more writing for the field of law? If not, is it possible for you to pursue it outside the bounds of your job? Once we started asking the right questions of possibilities, doors opened.

Curiosity is a powerful tool and mindset that helps us unravel all those questions that get tangled in our minds. But here's the thing—and it's why I mention curiosity often—because when you start getting curious, you can also start unraveling the why behind your unhappiness. That takes work and reflection, and it's often very scary. How come? Because that means you may have to do something about it.

Let's get curious about where you are now. Remember—and this is important—a curious mindset requires that you don't judge the answers. You're not assigning value or rebutting yourself with "but that won't work..." Instead, a curious mindset requires that you stay open to whatever comes up and tame your inner critic and that negative voice.

Not only that, but that you're also willing to sit with that critic and explore anyway.

Q: Without overthinking, what would you list as your current values? (Examples: family, flexibility, etc.)

Q: Now, let's dive deeper into your current reality and examine your day-to-day in your personal and professional life. When you reflect on that and determine what you prioritize and give your time and attention to, what comes up as the values, based on those priorities?

Q: Do they match up with the first list?

My definition of ambition used to be similar to my definition of success—put in the hours, take on more work, move up the ladder, and prove that you want it. Success was the result, and ambition was the catalyst, right?

It took me years to unravel why I valued ambition in this way. When I found the answer (which was that it was more out of societal and cultural conditioning), I didn't *remove* ambition as a value—as it's an important part of my identity—but I did redefine it. This happened over years of experimentation, seeking out mentors, trying to find my place and understanding, and also being okay that ambition can look different than what's been modeled for us.

In my late twenties and early thirties, I worked hard to excel at work. I pleased my bosses, I put in all the hours, and I took on the big projects with enthusiasm, even if I wasn't truly excited. Then, as I got older and more evolved, I longed to have a more integrated life with my kids. And here's the "aha!" I realized that neither of those approaches were less ambitious. And I felt so much freedom and clarity in owning my own definition of success! As I told my manager when I left my corporate job, *I am ambitious not just for my work, but for my whole life.*

AN INTEGRATED, VALUE-DRIVEN SCHEDULE

You may be wondering how all that curiosity paid off for me. Well—it's drastically shifted how I shape my day and the priorities that lead my schedule. Here's a glimpse of what my daily life looks like in this season: what's most important is that there's a fluidity to my schedule. Sometimes, I spend more time with the kids. Other times, I spend more time with work. If I anchor too far one way or the other, that's okay. I will adjust accordingly. What's true though is that my core anchor is always my values. And when your values and priorities align in your day-to-day, now that's magic!

Here's an example of my integrated schedule that is in alignment with this season of my life.

- Do the morning routine with the kids and drop them off at school (Value: family)
- Go to yoga, spin class, or Pilates (or some form of exercise) three to four times a week (Value: wellness)
- Meditate (Value: mental wellness and spirituality) on the mornings I don't exercise or feel extra tense
- Work with clients/administrative work/strategy work (Values: doing work that lights me up, relationships, ambition, freedom, curiosity, creativity)
- Have lunch with clients or friends (Values: relationships, authenticity, freedom)
- Pick up kids (Value: family)
- Drive to after-school sports and activities and cheer

on the kiddos when I can (Value: family, wellness, new experiences)

- Have dinner together as a family (Value: family, wellness)
- Do night routine, which consists of one of the following, not all three—work (sometimes), watch television, spend time with partner (Value: family, relationships)
- Turn the lights out! (Value: wellness, freedom)
- Not having to ask anyone for permission about taking time to be with my kids or at any of their activities during the school day or taking time off and just being where I want to be! (Total FREEDOM and worth everything!)

This fluid schedule is far more rewarding because it's rooted in what matters most to me. Your schedule will look different. How exciting and energizing will it be to discover what that can look like for you?

I shared my list of values with you in this chapter. If making this list for yourself isn't intuitive, that's okay! I'm here to help.

If you're having trouble determining your priorities, something that's helped my clients is to start with a top-down approach; find your values first and use those as guideposts. I have compiled a list of common values to help you do just that. The A to Z resource is free and available in full at www.soheejunphd.com/resources/.

....

....

....

....

As you work through the following exercise, remember that it's not about "boiling the ocean," and it's not about getting it perfect. Instead, slowly peel back the onion and find a handful that feel undeniably true for you. Once you've identified your current key values, ask yourself how they're being played out today—and what it would look like if they were more at the forefront of your future.

If looking at a list of words above in the Common Values Whittling Exercise doesn't appeal to you, try a visual approach. I know I'm more visually inclined, so this one works well for me. I've also used this approach with many of my clients in the entertainment, media, and startup industries. Sometimes, there's just more appeal to cutting and pasting vs. making lists!

It's likely that you've heard of a vision board, but this modern spin is specific to helping you find your values and priorities in a different way than a list of one hundred values can.

1. First, start to collect photos (either on the web, in magazines, or both) that resonate with you, that give you energy, or simply make you happy or feel grounded when you look at them. Now, this is important: don't place any judgment on what you choose. There are no right and wrong photos here—just the guidelines I've already shared. Once you have a pile of photos, cut out the ones that feel most important first, and affix them to your vision board. Don't overthink this part! Let it happen naturally. You'll also want to cluster photos that are alike. For example, if you have many photos of people working out, exercising, and doing physical things, cluster those photos together on the board, and so on.

2. When you've got the entire board filled in, step back and look at it critically for the first time. Can you identify any patterns or themes in the clusters? Did you choose several photos that show travel, for example? Community? Friendships? The purpose is to bring to your eye what your values are if the traditional list feels too stuffy.

On my vision board, for example, I have a Zen Buddha in the center who appears peaceful and is radiating light, evidence of my value on mental wellness and priorities of meditation and spirituality. I placed it in the center because it's core to me. What will be in the center of your board?

....

....

....

I often ask my coaching clients to think of what they love to do and are passionate about in terms of energy. People often mistake passion for only those things they enjoy and that comes easily, but this isn't always true. When you're passionate and naturally inclined at something, even a difficult task(s), they can still give you energy and a sense of fulfillment even if you're "tired." Those activities and things that drain us, or take away our energy, are usually things that we can do but don't necessarily want to do, enjoy doing, or are naturally good at doing.

Try to get as specific as possible here.

1. What gives you energy in your work?

....

....

....

....

2. What gives you energy in your life?

....

....

....

....

3. What takes away energy from your work?

....

....

....

....

4. What takes away energy from your life?

....

....

....

....

5. Get curious here. Remember not to judge yourself or say, "that isn't possible because..." Stay open and imagine, revisiting your list of values that you completed. Reflecting on that list, if you could design a work situation and a life that fuels and energizes you, what would it look like?

....

....

....

....

6. Now, take it a step further and get as detailed as possible, even writing about your ideal "day in the life" or week.

....

....

....

....

WHAT'S NEXT?

By now, you have a handle on your values and priorities—or, at the least, you're having a meaningful conversation with yourself about what those look like for you. That's huge, especially if you've never looked at your life in this macro way before. Good work!

In the next chapter, we'll tackle something that probably feels even bigger, especially for us ambitious women. It's time to take back control over the stories we tell ourselves, and we can start by rethinking risk and fear.

CHAPTER THREE

Rethinking Risk
and Fear

———

"When one door closes, another opens. But the hallway is a bitch."

—UNKNOWN

Six months after I left my corporate job, I had a moment of pure joy. It felt like I was living the quote I wrote down so long ago, "Happiness is when your expectations become reality." I distinctly remember writing a thought in the gratitude section I created on my iPhone that stated, "I feel so much gratitude for this life. I am living the life I imagined for myself and my family, being the boss of my time and not having to ask for permission. To me, that's everything, and I'm grateful for that."

Okay, don't get me wrong, I didn't feel that way because hundreds of clients were knocking down my door, or because my kids were angels, always super happy and didn't fight, or because it was like the end of a romance movie in which we cue to an utterly perfect and happy ending. In spite of those things being true....the bickering of my kids, the desire to win more client work, and the daily challenges, I still felt a sense of peace and calm. It *was* because I felt integrated into the fabric of my kids' lives while creating work that gave me energy and spending my time the way I wanted to. That, to me, was a success.

All that, thanks to taking a risk. But, of course, getting there is never easy.

THE MIND AND BODY'S RESPONSE TO RISK AND FEAR

Let's get real! We've been socialized and conditioned to think of risk as a bad thing. As something to stay away from. As something that's scary or hard. The word comes with a hefty side of the possibility of loss, injury, or peril, and lots of bad shit!

I call BS! Risk, on its own, is a neutral word. *We're* (society and us, as individuals) the ones who have assigned it meaning. In today's modern world, the risks we take are more likely to give us bruised egos or cause embarrassment than to do real, lasting physical harm.

The good news is that means we can be the ones who take it back.

One of the most important tools I use as a coach is to reframe risk for my clients by guiding them to look at the word through the lens of experience. Whatever you do next—whatever "risk" you take—it's just earned experience. It's adding to your collective context of the world and how to exist within it and more importantly, data for what you want to do next.

This vantage point and reframe works, and for good reason. I passionately believe that we make the best decisions we can at any given time using the information we have at that time. That's all risks are, at the end of the day: choices. *Experiences.* I coach my clients—and, now, I'm coaching you—to make these decisions boldly. Then, use their outcomes as data to make your next choice.

I know what you're thinking...

But, Sohee, what about the fear associated with risk? It's not that easy to just shut off.

And you'd be right. It's normal to experience a physical response to even thinking about taking a risk and the associated fear. You are not alone in it, at all! Remember the story I shared of me just thinking about leaving my job and how I was literally sweating!? That's a real fear response! Yet, it helps to take a step back and sit with the fact that most people feel this way. Knowing that takes some of the sting away.

Ever heard of the amygdala hijack? The amygdala is an almond-shaped set of neurons located deep in the brain's medial temporal lobe. That's to say, it's a tiny but powerful part that's very deep in our brain! It plays a key role in the processing of emotion. And is indeed scary especially when our amygdala, otherwise known as our "lizard brain," gives off a fight or flight response to stimuli or an event or situation. In prehistoric times, that response was useful. It could save you from, say, literally getting eaten by bears or a cheetah—you get the picture. Today, though, that same response goes off anytime we feel threatened or perceive danger, especially in a social context such as the workplace. The primitive part of our brain wants to protect you, but it can sometimes do more harm than good.

At the end of the day, the human condition is to seek out comfort and safety. Sometimes this serves us, and sometimes it does us a disservice. Once we get comfortable, there's an inertia that makes it hard to take action on the things that scare you. We want to stay comfortable, but that doesn't get you closer to an authentic life.

I asked my clients to do the same reframing around fear that they do with their association with the word *risk*. When we are fearful, it's typically because we don't want to fail. So, what does it mean to fail? What comes up for you when you think of failure? Can we reframe it to look at failure as a neutral word and that ultimately failure amounts to experiences? As more data for us to pivot in another direction?

What, then, do we do? If it's fear we're talking about, we can *use* it.

1. List all the words that come up when you think of the word "failure."

....

....

....

2. Now, list all the words that come up when you think of the word "experiences."

....

....

....

3. What can you do to start reframing how you perceive risk from failures to experiences?

....

....

....

FEAR AS A SIGNAL

Instead of signaling what you need to run *from*, fear could also be signaling the thing that you need to move *towards*— or at least what you need to look into more deeply. What matters most to us—what can have the largest area of impact—tends to elicit our biggest reactions or biggest amygdala hijacks!

For example, for two years before my partner and I had children, I ruminated on whether it was the right move. I talked to friends about it, trying to have my tribe convince me one way or the other. Trying to collect data on what it would be like, listing all the pros and cons and analyzing it line by line. It was such a fear-inducing, big risk for me, as it signified a huge change in the way we lived together, our identities as individuals, and our identity as a family. We were together ten years, as a duo, with no concerns other than growing our careers and figuring out how we wanted to spend our week-ends! Quite simply, it was a fear of the unknown. I mean, how would I be as a parent? How would he be? Would we be aligned? Would we have enough money? Would we be able to do the things we enjoyed as a twosome when we expanded that number? Did I want to lose the comforts of sleeping in and doing whatever we wanted, whenever we wanted? These were all the fears that came up for me, among other things, and it was huge all the way around. Big fears like this one tell us to pause and examine what's underneath them. Only by taking the big ball of fear apart can you start to make any sort of movement.

It happened again when I stepped out of being an individual contributor and moved to a management role back in my corporate job. It had been ten years since I had managed a team. Was I out of practice? Would I be good at it? Would they like me? Could I handle all the responsibilities that came with it? Did I even want to? What was holding me back? The fact that I was actually afraid didn't come to light until I paused and got curious about my reactions.

And, it's not just me. I coach people through fears quite often. I'm currently coaching a person who runs a company of 250 people. He has an underlying fear around really stepping into the role of the leader of the company. He's uncomfortable, nervous, and out of his comfort zone. I have encouraged him to unpack the roots of this fear one by one.

Why this step? Because it will serve him in other areas of his life, not just in the workplace.

If fears ever feel too cloudy, you can slice through the fog by asking one key question: "Are these fears grounded in truth?"

If the answer is no, use fear as a signal. Sometimes fear looms large because we look at it in one big, tangled ball/ mass. We go BIG in our fears! Acknowledge it, and choose to move forward by taking micro actions or the next best step to help tackle each fear and get past the inertia and desire to stay safe. Taking micro actions will help you get closer to your goals AND help you tune and strengthen your risk-taking muscles!

Sometimes, though, that can mean combatting another enemy along the way: your negativity bias.

NEGATIVITY BIAS

Sometimes, fear can stem from our negativity bias—which, trust me, is a real thing! Dr. Rick Hanson is well known for unpacking this for us and teaching us how we overlearn from negative experiences and fast-track to the memory of a negative experience, especially as women. As a psychologist and *New York Times* bestselling author, he speaks often about this bias and how it affects our choices in the present moment, which can prevent us from taking risks—big or small.

For example, say you once gave a presentation that bombed. Or you led a meeting that was a disaster—or maybe even didn't live up to your expectations, however slightly. Thanks to the negativity bias, instead of thinking, "I'll do better next time," you can over pivot by instead thinking, *Yeah, I'm not good at presenting,* or *I'm definitely never leading a meeting ever again.*

It's kind of like dating. If you have a few bad dates, you can feel like you're just not good at it in general. Not true! (And, newsflash, it probably wasn't all *you.* But that's a different book.)

Situations, however, are never black and white. There is never an all or nothing. In these moments, we should reflect on whether our reaction—which, again, is a pretty universal part of the human experience for women—is grounded in truth. Are you really a terrible presenter, or did you just have an off day? Is it true that you should never lead a meeting again, even though you've led many successful ones prior to the one that flopped? More importantly, what can we learn from these experiences so that we can move forward more confidently.

STRATEGIES TO RETHINK RISK AND FEAR

Next time you feel your negativity bias creeping up, take a pause and break it down. If after that you still have fear around the risk or action, that's completely understandable. Ask yourself what part, precisely, feels scary. Ask yourself what doing that scary thing would mean for your life and work. Pay attention to how you talk to yourself about what you're capable of, now and in the future.

Then if, after taking a pause, you make the decision that you do actually want to move forward, ask yourself what small or quick steps you can take. Write down two or three immediate next steps. These may seem tiny, but these micro actions are what will get you to that end state.

Then, extrapolate and expand on the plan. What micro actions can you take next week? In the next three weeks, next month? Choosing a tiered plan over your fear makes taking a risk feel more manageable. It's meant to unfreeze you and make it very manageable to move closer to your goals and dreams. It also prevents analysis paralysis, where your emotions and options can overwhelm you so much that you can't move at all.

MAKING A PLAN

A common fear women have around risk taking is that what works for someone else "just won't work for me." There's a perception that women who take risks and integrate their lives are "lucky." Or that they're "just different" or "special." That's not necessarily true; risk is work. It takes guts, yes. It also takes a belief that things could possibly work out better than you imagined, and it also takes planning and taking micro actions to get there. That's the hardest part, the act of putting to paper the steps you'll take to get you closer to your most integrated life.

Once, I was speaking to a teacher for two of my three kids who had recently made the switch from teaching full time to a job-share situation, in which she is in the school for two- and-one-half out of the five days.

"How did you make it happen?" I asked.

"I teach on Monday and Tuesday, and the other teacher and I both teach on Wednesday. Then, she takes over Thursday and Friday."

"Why did you decide to do this, and why now?"

"The kids are getting a bit older, with one entering junior high. They're facing different challenges. I want to be more available for them as they enter their teenage years."

I felt happy for her and could tell the adjustment was meaningful and value-aligned. The best kind of adjustment!

Later in our conversation, I learned it didn't just happen overnight. She had to think creatively both about the problem and how she may solve it.

She first enlisted the support of the co-teacher, and they cocreated a meaningful plan together, one that would work for both teachers AND benefit the school and kids! Once they felt solid in both their weekly schedule and were able to clearly articulate the benefits for the kids and school, they presented their proposal to the head of the school. The proposal articulated what the change would look like not just from *her* perspective, but from that of the organization. She made sure to share that they were getting two very experienced teachers for the price of one, and she also suggested they try it out for a year and then revisit how it was going for everyone.

With that compelling plan in place, the decision makers agreed—and now she's living her life in alignment! Doing so took a vision for what she wanted in this phase of her life and a plan of action. It also involved taking the risk, knowing that it could be turned down but understanding that it was the risk she needed to take for her family.

BUT WHAT ABOUT BIG RISKS?

You may be wondering how micro actions play out when it comes to big risks—those risks where you can't necessarily take baby steps. Maybe, for example, you're thinking of leaving your job, and you can't tiptoe out the door over the course of several months. That feels extra scary. Then what?

In these cases, go back to the reason why you considered the risk in the first place. Why did you start looking for another job? Why did you feel like you needed to take that step? What values or priorities were you trying to get closer to when you started the process? Will leaving this job accomplish that goal?

Next, take the sting out of it and reframe it. Often, especially as perfectionists, we trap ourselves in the permanence and stability of things. In reality, though, everything is always in flux. Our lives—within ourselves, our organizations, and the corporate world as a whole—are full of rapid change. If you're taking a big risk, remind yourself that it's simply a decision—one that *you can change* if it doesn't work. Nothing is permanent and it's just experience and data. Knowing you can pivot helps take the heat out of it.

Over anchoring into either/or thinking or our perfectionist tendencies makes it hard to take risks, but we also have the power to lift that anchor. Use it.

Similar to the other questions, take some time here to slow down. Let's find a comfortable place to sit back and reflect.

1. When was the last time you took a risk, big, small or somewhere in between that turned out well? How did that feel? What did you learn from taking that risk?

....

....

....

....

2. Think back to the life you envisioned and designed. What risks/actions would you take to get closer to making it a reality if you didn't care what people thought or you knew you couldn't fail?

....

....

....

....

3. Imagine that you succeeded in taking the risks you imagined in number 2. Get detailed here: What would that look like? More importantly: What would that feel like? What successes did you have?

....

....

....

....

4. Looking at your "day in the ideal life," what micro actions can you take now? List up to three micro actions you can take in the next few weeks.

....

....

....

....

We all have varying levels of tolerance for risk. Here, we'll take time to identify where you are on the risk scale. Looking at the graphic below, circle the number that fits you right now in terms of your level of risk tolerance.

Risk Meter

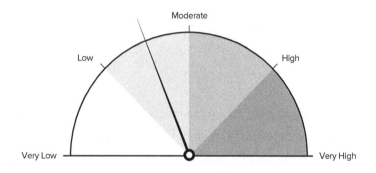

WHAT'S NEXT?

Rethinking risk and fear isn't a quick or easy process. Retraining your brain to respond differently to what scares you—especially when what scares you often feels big and unknown—takes time and practice. More than that, though, sometimes it requires giving yourself grace when things don't go the way you planned.

Which—hello!—can happen. A lot. That is, in fact, a core tenant of risk: facing the unknown, facing what you might not have a plan for. Terrifying, right?

I get it.

That's just one more reason why I'm such an advocate for self-care, as it helps in both this grace giving during times of stress and also on your day-to-day journey to living authentically. In the next chapter, we'll acknowledge why self-care can be so easy for women to bypass in today's world—and why, from here on out, that is no longer an option for you.

CHAPTER FOUR

Self-Care Is NOT an Option

"Self care is giving the world the best of you, instead of what's left of you"

—KATIE REED

In 2007, at the age of fifty-seven, my dad died unexpectedly in a horrific car accident. To say that it was devastating would be an understatement. He was so young and in good health...not something you would ever imagine happening. The grief that took over my mind and heart was immense, yet I felt a pull to go back to work. This was partly driven by the need to have the "distraction" of work, but it was mostly because I felt an internal pressure to go back. When I look back, I realize that I didn't give myself enough time and space to process the loss. At that time in my life, I was more unforgiving about how I showed up for work and "performed" every day, and I didn't allow the proper space for needing anything at all, let alone more time away from work. So, I took just two weeks off, and I went right back to the office—where grief would rise up in the most unexpected of times. I would find myself tearing up at my desk and in meetings. It would be fair to say that I was not productive, and I was in tears a lot. It definitely wasn't healthy. My bosses told me if I needed extra time, I should take it, but I felt I needed to be there. To be a good worker. To show my dedication and my value as an employee, at the expense of my own well-being.

As I was gutting it through, working while trying to keep my grief at bay, I began to suffer from stomach pains. I went to a gastroenterologist for help in diagnosing the problem. There in his office, I ticked off symptom after symptom. The last question he asked stuck with me, "Are you under any stress?"

Uhhh, yes I was! My work schedule was crazy-packed and oh yeah, my dad had just died.

"Stress manifests itself in the body," he told me. And wow, he was right. I wasn't allowing myself the space to grieve. I wasn't doing anything that could even resemble a therapeutic action, and my body was trying to tell me what it needed.

I was too busy diving into my work, giving to others, and making sure I was still "performing" in every area. I was making excuses for my lack of self-care—that is, until the stomach pains made me slow down. In hindsight, I was hiding from my feelings and the overwhelming sadness by diving into work, and my body didn't like it.

This is an extreme case, but the affliction-from-stress problem is a common one. Autoimmune disease is prevalent today, and stress and mentality of "gutting it through" for long periods of time is a key contributor, as is what you put in your body. The National Institutes of Health estimates over twenty-three million Americans suffer from autoimmune disease, and that number is increasing every year. But chances are, ten years ago you likely didn't know anyone who had Crohn's, IBS, or a similar disease. Women especially put a lot of pressure on themselves to be there for everyone and to keep all the plates spinning in the air, trying to keep this elusive balance going at any cost.

Often times, when we have children, it can be even harder to prioritize ourselves because we're constantly caregiving. This is where the excuses can creep up, double time. Sometimes, we will remedy our lack of self-care by leaning into our partners more and relying on them to fill the self void. This is a healthy benefit of having that deep relationship in your life—but only to a degree.

For example, when my dad died, sometimes my partner would go running with me. It was a sweet gesture. He knew

I needed something, but he didn't know how to help me. And that's okay. Sometimes, we need to find "that thing" outside of our family and friends that nourishes us, and we need to let it be ours alone.

Fast forward to 2019, as I was writing this book, my mom passed away after a tough battle with pancreatic cancer. It was heart-wrenching and unfamiliar, as I've never been through anything like that before. It was also very scary to watch someone you love whither away and not being able to control it or make it better for her. I was her primary caregiver, in the trenches with her day in and day out. Taking her to all of her appointments, making sure she ate, giving and getting her meds, being her companion, and just sitting with her, trying my hardest to bring some levity to a dire situation. During this time, I recall feeling so emotionally spent and completely untethered. As I cared for her, I also rediscovered the utter importance of caring for myself. At the start of this journey, my therapist adamantly pointed out that *I* needed to practice some form of self-care daily.

Daily? Seriously? I remember thinking. That sounds a little selfish. Who has the time? Who has the funds?

Even after having gone through the push and pull needs of self-care when my dad passed, it sounded extravagant, especially because before my mother got sick, I often put self-care last on my list because I felt like I simply didn't have the time. As you mamas know, when you have kids, it would be a luxury to have fifteen minutes of quiet time. The facial, the exercise class—when those ideas came up in conversation with other moms, the common refrain was "that must be nice." For the longest time, I felt that if I had that precious time, I should be spending it in a giving capacity, like reading a book to my kids, or putting extra time into my work. I was in that all-too-familiar cycle of constantly emptying my tank.

As I've coached more and more ambitious women, I've found I was in no way alone in this view of self-care. We'll unpack it more deeply later in this chapter.

In caring for my mother, though, I quickly came to re-realize that if I started to burn out, there was no way I could hold it together for anyone else. What I felt when I took a time-out was eye-opening. I became more present and aware of my surroundings and more balanced in my emotional state. I became grounded again.

Because it had been so long since my dad's death, I had to revisit my perception of self-care. It turned from one of self-indulgence and luxury to an absolute must. That in order to give to others, I had to give to myself first. To fill up my tank so that I can be of service. To be in service. To serve my kids, my mom, my work...all of it. I started slowly by taking an hour two or three mornings a week to go to yoga or Pilates because these exercises made me feel whole and physically grounded. I tried to schedule lunches at least twice a week with friends so that I could get out of my own context for a bit and connect to others. Feeling that sense of community and vibrancy did so much for me during this time in my life. When I started to feel like I was going into a slump or like I was about to spiral into my grief, it got me through. Some days, I quite literally didn't have the time or energy to do anything big, so I took a thirty-minute nap. And that counted as care.

Ultimately, taking time for myself actually made me more present for my children and my mom, who were going through the grieving process as well. Had I not practiced self-care, I would not have had the tank of emotional fuel to be there for them—all of whom needed me. My self-care routine didn't always keep that tank full, but it did help me replenish it so I could keep the car on the road and keep going day by day.

Your story undoubtedly looks different than mine. Even if you aren't caring for a dying parent, you surely have stressors—that's part of being human, and especially a woman in today's world. For all the benefits technology brings to our lives, one of the drawbacks is the need to always be on. This immersion with "the other" can give us less space to connect with ourselves, to create, to reflect. We need this space to regenerate and revive ourselves, and that's precisely the kind of space self-care delivers.

WHAT DO I MEAN BY "SELF-CARE?"

There's a lot of chatter today about self-care. In fact, the Global Wellness Institute (GWI) recently valued the wellness market at a whopping $4.2 trillion, having grown 12.8 percent in the last two years. That's huge! Let's be honest, though—with all that growth, it's still easy for ambitious women to think that sort of thing is for everyone but us. In this chatter, it's common to think of self-care as a cluster of activities that we would *like* to do, but not that we *have* to do. They're the things you can put on your list and bump if something more important comes up, right?

Wrong.

While yoga and facials are types of self-care, I prefer to look at it on the broader scope of overall wellness. There are five different realms of self-care: physical, psychological, emotional, social, and spiritual.

You define what activities fall under these realms. But it's important to take this broad view because we have so many dimensions to us. It's easy to just stay "on the surface" of self-care rather than being intentional and giving yourself what you really need. For me, **physical self-care** could look like any kind of movement or focus on the body that lights me up. During the time I was caring for my mom, it was so heavy and emotional at times that I felt a calling for lightness and fun. So, I got quiet and intentional about what that would look like, and it came to me: a beginner's hip-hop class! I love dancing of all forms and types, and because it gets me out of myself and into the moment, and it's just so much fun. So, I looked up classes, found one nearby, and took the class with a willing friend. It was just the lightness I needed.

Psychological self-care could look like taking the right medication or talking to the right psychologist. **Emotional self-care** could look like journaling or meditation. **Social self-care** could look like intentionally spending time with friends with whom I know I can honestly share my feelings or joining a support group. **Spiritual self-care** could be meditation or prayer. Prayer, by the way, doesn't have to be in church. I believe it is knowing what gives you meaning and faith in life, however that looks.

Some self-care activities will cross the spectrum. Whatever realm you need to focus more on in the moment is perfectly fine; there is no right answer. There is no "perfect balance"—that much we know for sure by this point. A date night with your partner or girls-night-in with your best friend, for example, could touch both social and emotional self-care. My approach to self-care isn't a rigid system, but rather one that helps you think about how you care for yourself with intentionality.

Intentionality in self-care, in fact, is the key to getting the most out of it.

When going through the loss of my mother, I had to lean very heavily into emotional and psychological self-care. I knew I needed to be mindful that if I spent all day with her caring for all of her needs as her primary caretaker, I needed to spend the next day caring for *my* emotional needs so that I could rebuild and refuel myself for the days ahead. Now, my self-care priorities look different, and that's okay. It's a different season. These days, I find that I need more social and spiritual self-care than anything else. I know that because I ask myself, "What do I need now?" This is a powerful coaching question that is useful to really tune into how you need to self-care.

However, the thread through the five realms, the one that ties everything together and makes self-care work, is this intentionality. Choose activities within those realms carefully. Budget your time for yourself like you budget your time for others. Apply that same kind of care and thought to the choices you make that will keep your tank full.

REFRAME SELF-CARE

If you feel like self-care is selfish—which, as I shared a moment ago, I used to as well—I encourage you to look deeply at why. Pause and think about that for a moment.

What is the underlying fear or perception for you that's not allowing you to prioritize yourself, even though you know you should? What are you afraid of losing? Who are you afraid of disappointing? What, if any, biases do you have around self-care?

These are not judgment questions, trust me.

If you are a perfectionist, you feel like you have to do the best absolutely every day, right? Drop that in general, but especially when you think about self-care. You don't have to be "all-in" in order to start. There is no magic threshold to reach and there is no finish line. As you saw from my examples with my dad and mom, there will be times in your life when your need for self-care will be urgent and absolutely necessary in order to maintain a sense of self. There will be other times when a manicure will do. The strategy is to honor where you are in your life and to listen to the body, because it's always talking to us. Our bodies are wise. In order to live a big, fulfilled life, self-care is the foundation from which you'll build. Guilt and the negative associations we have around putting our oxygen mask on first doesn't serve us in the long run. We are wired for rest and need it to perform at our best.

If it's been forever since you've gone to the gym, had your nails done, or sat on a meditation mat, it can legitimately feel overwhelming to know where to start. I know it did for me at times. Here's the playbook. Start by asking yourself, "What do I need *now?*" Once you've asked yourself that, allow for quiet and honor what arises.

After you've quieted down and you've tuned in, choose a micro action for the next day, the next week, the next month. If you think maybe you should talk to a therapist but you've never been in therapy before, for example, the fear around that act of self-care can be overwhelming. Pick a small step instead; set a goal to do your research on the therapists in your area. Then, set a goal to talk to one of your girlfriends who has experience with therapy and can help you understand what to expect. Then, set another goal to set up your initial appointment. Now, instead of one giant goal that can feel scary and hard, you have a series of micro actions that are, in themselves, acts of self-care.

PAUSE POINT

Q: What do you need now in terms of self-care?

THE EXCUSES ANTIDOTE: ACTION

Here's the thing: If you want to live a life that energizes you, self-care is not an option. It's the means by which you can maintain and sustain your life and be there for others. If you're on the fence about where to start when it comes to self-care, I recommend prioritizing the mental side of wellness over physical, in the beginning. Try a five-minute meditation, or simply take some deep breaths, perhaps check out your local yoga class, or actively step away from the guilt associated with self-care. Much like we removed the negative connotation of risk from our vernacular and reframed what risk is in the last chapter, we can do the same here for self-care.

Untangle "selfish" and "self-care," right now. Above all else though, actively reframe the guilt and the negative voices that may crop up in your head when you are thinking of doing something beneficial for yourself. Much like we removed the negative connotation of risk from our vernacular in the last chapter, we can do the same here for self-care.

WORKBOOK: REFLECTION QUESTIONS

The following are from Mary McCoy, LMSW, a licensed social worker:

1. What do I most enjoy doing with my time? (Your answer shouldn't include work or chores.)

....

....

....

....

2. What activities make my heart feel at rest and at peace?

....

....

....

....

3. When do I feel the most full of life and well-being?

....

....

....

....

4. When do I feel the tension release from my neck, shoulders, and jaw? What am I doing when this tension goes away?

....

....

....

....

5. Which people provide me with energy, strength, and hope, and how much time do I spend with them compared to the people who drain my sense of well-being with negativity and guilt?

....

....

....

....

6. When do I feel my life is full of purpose and meaning?

....

....

....

....

Take thirty minutes—right now—to pause and reflect on the five realms of self-care. How would you rank yourself, from one to five, in terms of how satisfied you feel in each of them? Remember, there is no right answer or perfect score.

Satisfaction Scale

1	2	3	4	5
Very Dissatisfied	Dissatisfied	Neutral	Satisfied	Very Satisfied

Physical ....

Psychological ....

Emotional ....

Social ....

Spiritual ....

Next, look at your rankings. In what areas can you give yourself more attention and energy? Which realm feels most true to you to explore in this moment, and what are your ideal activities within it?

....

....

....

Sit with these questions—without judgment—and develop a micro action plan. I bet you'll feel lighter right away.

....

....

....

....

Ask yourself: What can you do in the next three days, three weeks, and three months?

....

....

....

....

WHAT'S NEXT?

Many people don't understand the value of self-care until they're pushed to the edge, as I have been. My hope is that with the reflections and tools in this chapter, you realize that it doesn't have to be true for you. That you can see the benefits of self-care and the power of taking small steps in that direction.

Slow down. You can take one step, however small, today. I will walk with you.

Now, we understand that self-care makes us better versions of ourselves. Those best versions of ourselves are more equipped to tackle what we're going to cover in our next chapter: making authentic choices throughout the changing seasons of our lives.

CHAPTER FIVE

Making Authentic Choices from Season to Season

———

"Advice is what we ask for when we already know the answer but wish we didn't."

—ERICA JUNG

You should be a doctor.

You should be a dermatologist.

You should be a dentist.

As a young woman—especially a young Asian woman growing up in a household with high expectations—I had many family members who constantly and intentionally handed me a list of "should-bes" for my life. And whether I liked it or not, I took all these should-bes in, consciously and unconsciously. They were my formal and informal roadmaps for what was acceptable, what was expected, and the framework from which I should decide my future life.

So, not surprisingly, in college, I went gung-ho in the pursuit of a medical degree. Ta-da! I was going to be a doctor! Was I passionate about the sciences? Mmm, not really. Was I interested in the medical field? Honestly, no. Not outside of the prestige it would bring me and the accolades and respect I would get from my family.

Still, I went through the rounds: organic chemistry, all the prerequisites required for a student to advance into medical school. So far so good, smooth sailing. Then, something happened in my third year of college: I failed Physics 101. FAILED! For a student who had never failed in her life before, this was BIG and terrifying! Who me? Overachieving, perfectionistic Sohee...fail? Yes—and thankfully it was at this time that I decided to slow down, to reexamine my college path thus far, and get really honest with myself. Did I fail because I didn't like the subject and/or the field of medicine, or was it something else? When I gave myself some time to breathe, slow down, and get off the prescribed path, it came to me:

I don't know if this is something I want to do, I thought. Which was a big deal.

Prior to that, I'd even job-shadowed a dentist. That didn't feel right, either. (Nothing against dentists, but I didn't want to stick my fingers into people's mouths every day.)

I felt stuck. I felt scared. I knew I had to make a decision, and I knew that decision would alter the course of my adult working life—a feeling of anxious dread many twenty-somethings have likely experienced.

Given this experience, I decided to explore my senior year classes with much more curiosity. Reading through the course descriptions, I saw it: Industrial Organizational Psychology! This was a course that blended psychology with the workplace. Back in those days, it was a field that was still up-and-coming, and as a psych major, I found it fascinating to explore non-clinical applications of psychology.

This sounds interesting, I thought. It meets my desire to help people with the working world. I'll sign up!

From day one of that class, I lit up! Everything about it was a "yes" for me!

This was a turning point in my life where I went in the direction of what felt right instead of following the slew of "shoulds" that were hammered into me from very early on. It was risky, though. It was a burgeoning field, not yet fully blown, and there weren't many colleges giving master's or

PhDs in it. I didn't have any role models in the field outside of my professors. I knew I could teach with the degree, but other practical examples felt up in the air. I was moving away from the tried-and-true doctor/dentist route—with all those fancy, shiny credentials—to a field that was still relatively untested and that not many companies knew about.

Despite the risk, when I tuned into what my inner voice was telling me, I knew it was right. But it wasn't easy.

I tried to explain the field to my parents—who were immigrants and heavily invested in the education of their second daughter going through college—but even they didn't understand. There were no words in the Korean language at that time to describe the role, but I tried. In making this shift, I had to do away with the assumptions and biases that were all around my situation, many of them cultural. I felt like I was coming into my own and like it was something I definitely had to do.

And I'm so glad I did!

That singular choice to slow down and reexamine my choices started me on the path I am on today, and I am grateful not only for those inner signals, but for my strength that allowed me to listen to them.

As seasons change, our signals aren't always going to be

as grand as the one in my example. We won't always be smacked with light bulb moments right when we need them. Most of the time, these inner signals that lead us to making authentic choices are much smaller. A move could feel like the right step. It could feel interesting and energizing. You could have a curiosity around it that you just can't shake—these are signals, too.

We can see them if we remain curious and open.

THE TRAP OF SOCIALIZING YOUR DECISIONS

As women, we need to give ourselves permission to turn into our inner signals. This can be especially challenging when you consider our propensity to try to socialize our decisions instead—to ask others what they think we should do. This is often because, while we can sometimes recognize these signals, we haven't learned to trust ourselves enough to listen to them. We look for others to tell us it's okay.

I want to be clear: it's natural to ask for feedback, and feedback can indeed be helpful. What we want to avoid, though, is giving away our power by letting that feedback direct our action(s) *when it's in opposition to our intuition, to our gut.* Other people—friends, family, colleagues—can be well-intentioned, but they are offering opinions based on the lens through which they see the world and it doesn't include your life context and your unique experiences.

As women, we're biologically wired to need a tribe. We're socialized that way. In prehistoric times, men and women had clear-cut roles: men would do the hunting, and women would stay in the village, cooking, and caretaking, surrounded by other women who were doing the same. These women weren't required to use their physical bodies as much as the men, and they banked more on their emotional and social skills. They had to work together to tend to the fields, to care for the kids, to provide a safe village. These women were conditioned to hone into their social abilities, to get along. If you were an outlier in these times, a free-thinker without a tribe, you likely would not survive.

This reliance on tribe has been ingrained in us, hardwired generation to generation. Even back then, men and boys took the risks, and women and girls played nice to get along. That is true even today; in and out of the workplace, women still lean into their social skills. We often don't have as much overt power and control—looking at the larger society in general—as men do. We're still not on an equal playing field, no matter how many advancements have been made. This is a large factor into why we look to our tribe out of a deep-rooted tendency toward agreeableness. We turn to our community and our friends for support, but also unconsciously for them to answer a key question: "Is this okay?" We don't want to unnecessarily ruffle feathers. We don't want to be an outlier. We want to survive, and we want our tribe.

We also globalize this tribe, making it bigger in our minds. When we're trying to make an authentic choice, thinking of "the women who are looking up to us," (or those who rely on us, or...the list goes on) we can make an already-big decision feel that much weightier. The feeling gets huge in our heads and our hearts when we focus outward on all the people we could potentially disappoint or hurt with our choices. I know this because I've lived it; I used to ask my friends for advice all the time. I wanted to know what they thought I should do at particular times in my life, what move they thought I should make next. If they were thinking of having kids, if they thought I should stay in the job, if they thought I was making a good or bad move (of any kind). And more often than not, it left me even more confused.

In the book, *Playing Big*, by Tara Mohr, she writes that most of the feedback you'll receive is not important to integrate into your work. This is especially true for women innovators, change agents, and activists. Much of the feedback is backlash or people feeling threatened by or not understanding the ideas. Some reflect attachments to the "usual way" of doing things. What you should think about instead is: *What feedback do I need to incorporate in order to be effective in reaching my aims? And what feedback really won't impact my effectiveness and is okay to ignore?*

Here's an example: I'm mentoring a woman who is in the same field as I am, and she isn't happy with her role. This has her second-guessing her choice to have entered the field of learning and development at all. We were having a conversation one day in which she explained at length the stress she's feeling in her current role. So much so that she's having physical symptoms like massive stomach aches, body aches, her shoulders hurt, she had headaches and all-around body pains! She then told me about a role that's open in her organization that she's interested in where the team seems really great. And the role, while not directly related to her current one, seemed interesting. Then she did it. She asked me, "Should I apply for the role? Do you think I'm making the wrong decision?"

We do it all the time. Knowingly and unknowingly. My guidance to her was to follow her intuition and that while it might feel scary, she could always change course if, in fact, she did get the new role. In the meantime, she needed to make a move to care for her immediate physical issues. I advised that she visit her doctor for her physical symptoms and to really tune into what she felt was the next best micro step for her career.

The problem arises when we lean too much into the tribe looking for answers when we truly know, deep down, what those answers are. When we get still and cut through the noise, we can hear ourselves. We can tune in to what our inner compass is telling us. Then, when we meet with our tribes, we find ourselves having a different and more fruitful conversation. There's a distinct difference in asking for support based on the decision you've made and asking your support system to make that decision for you.

As Erica Jung famously quipped, "Advice is what we ask for when we already know the answer but wish we didn't." She's right.

WHAT IF YOU FEEL STUCK?

The choices I made before I had kids are different than the choices I've made since, and that's okay. They were all authentic to me in those contexts.

If you're stuck in decision-making paralysis, ask yourself something: Are you afraid of making the wrong move? If so, start with the inverse. If you're ambitious, are you afraid of staying still? What would happen if you *didn't* make a change? How fulfilled would you be? What does the status quo look like for you this time next year? If you're comfortable with that, maybe it's authentic for you to stay where you are. If you're not comfortable with that—if checking the temperature on future you feels depleting instead of energy-giving—that's a signal.

Whatever choice you do or don't make, one fact remains: you won't be here forever. You can change your mind. Remind yourself of that, every day if you have to. You have the power to make an authentic choice that fulfills you. You have permission to ask yourself what gives you energy.

But...what if you don't know what gives you energy? What if you're so stuck that even that feels too big?

I have a friend—we'll call her Jamie—who has an Ivy League education and opted to leave her career to stay home and care for her children, one of whom has special needs. At the time she made that decision, it was the right one. Today, though, after spending eight years in mommyville, she's ready to add something new to her day-to-day. The problem? She's been so engrossed in mommy duties that she doesn't have any clue what to do. She doesn't know what she's passionate about. Going back to the analytical role she had prior to kids doesn't feel fulfilling anymore. She feels the work world has advanced too far and she doesn't know where to start. She feels completely stuck.

To compound the matter, Jamie is a highly analytical person and lives for plans—a trait I think is admirable in many ways. Still, she's in her head a lot, and she has a hard time unlocking what's next unless she has a clear-cut answer or set of steps. The problem? There are no set of steps to reach a destination you can't pinpoint. Getting unstuck is about possibilities. I live in that space of possibilities and visioning, and for my clients—and friends like Jamie—I help them utilize that tool, too, to bring them closer to their goals—whatever they are.

I asked Jamie some of the reflection questions I'll ask you at the end of this chapter, encouraging her to imagine her life a year from now and then work backward to identify micro actions that would lead her there. In Jamie's case, "there" was merely having clarity on the "what." Sometimes, when you're that stuck, it can take a long while before you move into the "how."

In six months to a year, Jamie hopes to have identified one or two hobbies that she's curious about or one or two part-time jobs she could pursue that gives her energy. That's it. And that's enough. For now.

PAUSE POINT

The guidance I gave my friend, and what I'll share with you, is to really examine the following questions:

1. Going back to the answers around what gives and depletes your energy, what possibilities are open to me?

....

....

2. What activities are you curious about? What hobbies, roles, and jobs have you been curious about before?

....

....

....

....

This isn't always intuitive. Do you ever notice how when you're doing something you're not jazzed about, it depletes your energy? I recall early on in my career, I was working for a very detail-oriented manager. I had to do every task with laser-like precision and lay out step-by-step detailed project plans for every event and every meeting or workshop we planned. What I knew was that I could do it and do it well...but it depleted my energy every time I did. At the end of every "detail deep-dive plan," I felt spent! No more energy left.

If you've felt that, tune into that feeling. Examine those

things that give you energy! For me, coaching professionals makes me feel energized and alive, no matter how tough the session gets. And teaching makes me feel so energized—even after a long eight-hour marathon teaching session. Once you notice what gives you energy vs. depleting you, follow that. Take it one step further and do more of it or explore how to expand it. Get curious!

STILL WORK TO DO

This process of tuning into yourself and being authentic is an ever-evolving process. It isn't one and done. Anytime there's a change in your life circumstance or situation big or small, you'll naturally want to "fit in" and play to the crowd. Perhaps play smaller than you normally do. That's a normal part of reforming. However, the more you're aware of this, the faster you can start to make authentic choices that are true for your unique life and to own it!

Recently, I reflected on how I was showing up in a mom's group I joined. Initially, I had been careful not to appear too ambitious. I had been hiding that part of me, hesitating to volunteer for tasks I normally would have, avoiding discussing successes at work, not mentioning I was working on a book, and so on. I didn't want to look like I was "too much" for the group. Essentially, I was hiding parts of myself in order to fit what I thought was the appropriate persona for the context, for the tribe.

When I got still and examined this behavior, I asked myself what felt authentic to me in this context—and whether or not I was living that out. I decided I needed to be more transparent with my work wins within the group. I wanted to share what was happening on all sides of my life. Would they think I was too ambitious? Too extra? Too whatever? If they did, I decided I would be completely okay with it. It took awareness and observation to reach this decision, but when I did, I felt so much lighter.

This is proof that I don't have it all figured out. Even as an executive coach for strong women, showing up authentically in *my* life and making choices that are true to *my* context is still sometimes a challenge, and it always will be. That's life. And that's okay.

The Fulfillment Scale we worked through in chapter one is not a one-time assessment. Every six months at a minimum, revisit the following questions and rank them on a scale from one to five.

Fulfillment Scale

(1)	(2)	(3)	(4)	(5)
Extremely Unfulfilled	Unfulfilled	Neutral	Fulfilled	Extremely Fulfilled

How fulfilled are you in your role as a mother? ....

How fulfilled are you in your role as a partner? ....

How fulfilled are you spiritually? ....

How fulfilled are you physically? ....

How fulfilled are you emotionally? ....

How fulfilled are you mentally? ....

How fulfilled are you in your career? ....

Use your honest ratings to these questions to help you navigate whether or not it's time to make a shift, however small. Consistently reevaluating how you feel forces you to look inward—something that's especially helpful in a world full of distractions. It helps you face yourself in a targeted, productive way.

I still use this tool today. Recently, I found that while being a solo-preneur was rewarding in many ways, I missed the rich ideas and energy that I got through partnerships and collaboration. I took that information as a push to partner with people on projects as much as possible, giving me more fulfillment in my career as a solo business owner. Catching this early (courtesy of the Fulfillment Scale) helped me prevent burnout down the line and live a more fulfilled life.

Don't be afraid to look inward. That's where the answer often lies.

Again, let's get really curious and open-minded here, keeping in mind your collective responses in the Fulfillment Scale, the values you identified, the priorities, and your day in the life vision:

1. What risk(s) are you thinking of taking?

....

....

....

....

2. Is there fear? If so, name the fear.

....

....

....

....

3. What would happen in your work and life if you didn't make the change/take the risk?

....

....

....

....

4. What could happen if you did? What possibilities would open up as a result?

....

....

....

....

5. Imagine that you did take the risk identified in question one. Envision the best case scenario upon taking the risk. In great detail, describe what your life would then look like in all aspects: work, family, social, spiritual, emotional, and physical.

....

....

....

....

6. With that detail in mind, what are the one to three micro actions you can take in the next three days, three weeks, and three months to get you closer to the vision you hold? Get specific here with the actions.

....

....

....

....

WHAT'S NEXT?

If you're having trouble making the next move, I'm not here to blame or shame you. You're a product of the society we live in—we all are—and this is a safe space in which I'm trying to undo some of that conditioning.

If you walk away from this book committed to living with more intentionality and feeling empowered to define your own mommytrack, I will have done my job. In the conclusion of our journey, we'll work through the final piece: not just redefining risks for ourselves, but taking them.

CHAPTER SIX

Taking the Right Risks—Right Now

———

"Leap and the net will appear."

—ZEN SAYING

Today, all my wins and all my learnings have amounted to information about what did and did not feel right to me in any given season. Note I used the word learning instead of failure, and that's totally on purpose. It's all data I can use to prepare me for how to best take my next steps. When you shift your perspective in this way, risks don't feel so scary; they just feel like part of life, a data point, experience.

I'M NOT DONE

Today in my life, I feel fully integrated. I'm more present and engaged with my kids, and I'm managing a business I love—one that brings me energy and that I'm able to lean into without feeling depleted. I'm able to pivot and adjust when I need to, continually reevaluating where I am and where I want to go. I feel in flow, and my day-to-day is aligned with my values and priorities.

It takes work, though, and that doesn't mean my life is all figured out. For example, with the recent passing of my mom, I've got a new set of challenges around childcare, which was an integral part of my feeling supported. I need to find a new person I trust to help pick up the kids when I can't, to be there when both my partner and I are occupied with work, and so on. We're not trying to be perfect; we're trying to stay in continuous communication and do the work to make *us* work in the next season of our lives.

I'm also evolving my business constantly. And, while some pieces of it do, of course, still feel like obligations, they are obligations I can handle because they're part of something larger—something I want and that is, again, tied to my values.

I am constantly assessing where I am and asking what I need to do to honor my mental and physical self. Cultivating a mindset of curiosity has benefited me greatly in this respect, as has my client work. Both require flexibility and introspection. I'm the first person to tell you that yes, I've gone to therapy. And I continue to do the work. I'm proud of that, and it's a work in continuous progress. That's the fun!

SHE'S NOT DONE

A former colleague—we'll call her Ari—found herself in a similar situation to the one I found myself in all those years ago. She grew up in a high-pressure culture and was chasing the societal ideal of looking outwardly successful. She sought the promotions, the advancements. Eventually, she was working as the team lead on technical change management projects for a large media conglomerate. That ladder we all know? She was climbing it and fast.

Inwardly, though, she was in turmoil. What she really wanted was to make a difference with people and work in more one-on-one scenarios. She felt that the additional responsibility took her further from that ideal. She was doing work that was more *im*personal when she wanted it the other way around.

Ari was miserable, crying a lot and generally unhappy. It started to creep into her performance too, and she made a mistake in a large-stakes meeting with senior executives from across many business units because her heart just wasn't in it.

Ari knew that there was another department—the one I happened to work in at the time—that was more in line with what she loved and what gave her energy. She was curious, and she took the micro action to job shadow me one day to see what it was like. Ultimately, the pain she felt in doing work she wasn't passionate about outweighed the risk she'd be taking. And it was a huge risk—yet it was the right risk for her. When the opportunity came up, she left her old role to start on the "ground floor" of that new department, leaving behind a high-ranking title and position in the change management team to gain experience in the area she wanted to pursue.

For Ari, she determined that what she wanted from her career wasn't all about title—it was about making a difference. She discovered this through reflection and was able to capitalize on it by flexing her risk-taking muscle. She gave herself permission to question her definition of success, and she blossomed because of it!

Sometime in the future, Ari may get curious about another path, and that's okay. She's not done.

YOU'RE NOT DONE

I mention my story and Ari's story here not for comparison purposes, but to reinforce that there is no end to this journey. Your goal is to be in alignment with what matters to you in this season of your life. Your goal is to feel integrated, to feel full. To listen to those inner signals and act on them. To make your own mommytrack, the one that's headed where you want it to go.

If you're not sure where to start, I encourage you to get curious. If you're scared, the best action to take is to feel that fear. Sit with it and get even more curious about the fear. Pause. Then, make a plan and move toward those micro actions you know I'm such a proponent of. Understand that risk-taking is an ebb and flow, just like life. You *can* change your mind. Making intentional choices and taking actions based on the information you have now all adds to experiences (not failures). Be proud that you've come this far in the journey. And guess what? You're not done.

WORKBOOK: REFLECTION QUESTIONS

1. What's coming up for you now as we get close to the end of our journey?

....

....

....

....

2. What's been the best discovery for you up to this point?

....

....

....

....

3. What's resonated the most with you up to this point?

....

....

....

....

4. Take a look back on all of your answers to the Reflection
   Questions. What's been surprising for you?

....

....

....

....

Take a moment to list your values, priorities, and risk options as well as the answers to the Fulfillment Scale. Pay attention to how it feels in your body when you write out these potential risks. Which are the scariest? Why? Spend some time there.

Then, complete the following Risk Meter that we came to know in chapter three, gauging your tolerance for actually taking a risk now. Has it changed? There's no reason to pad these answers—like everything else, there's no perfect score. Be honest.

Risk Meter

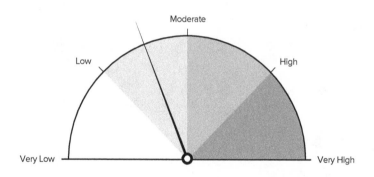

Now, you can clearly see your risk options and your risk tolerance. Can you create a list of micro actions in alignment with your endgame? Can you take that first step? By reading this far and completing this exercise, I'd say you already have.

....

....

....

....

Conclusion

———

"Be patient with yourself. Self-growth is tender; it's holy ground. There's no greater investment."

—STEPHEN COVEY

We've been on quite a journey together, haven't we? My hope is that you found the chapters of this book engaging and thought provoking.

Now, it's time to take action!

Know that this "action" will look different to everyone, but here's a constant: whatever you do, don't ask someone else what you should do. Don't give away your power. Don't socialize your decisions or your definition of success. Those are yours.

Are you going to speak to your boss about a flexible work schedule? Are you looking at stepping off the corporate treadmill and exploring the creative side of you and creating a product? Do you feel an urge to start your own company? Do you feel compelled to take on bigger and more visible projects at work? Do you feel excited by the thought of putting your name in for that big promotion at work?

Whatever you choose, give yourself a due date and write down micro actions (look at the next three days, three weeks, and three months) to help you get there. If you feel like you need more support, tell a trusted colleague or friend about your plans. (Note that I said *tell* them, don't ask them if it's a good idea or not. There's a distinct difference.)

And even after all that...yes, you may still fail. But that's okay, because you'll have taken a risk and gained crucial experiences to help you make the next best decision for you. You'll have learned and gathered data you can use for your next move—a move that will feel easier and may even stick. Embrace these learning moments. I need you to hear me when I say we all need to be very careful about perfectionism and people pleasing creeping in. There's no room for that if we want to live authentic lives.

I also wouldn't be authentic and true if I didn't share that in the journey of writing this book, my personal situation intentionally shifted in a monumental way. My partner, my husband of nineteen years, and I made the brave decision to divorce and part ways. In the midst of this journey to unravel nineteen years of habits, finances, and more and forge a new partnership and way forward, we are also facing the life-altering COVID-19, social distancing experience.

It would be a serious understatement to say that there's global anxiety. It's a scary time for all, and really not an ideal time to get a divorce. (Not that there is ever an 'ideal' time!) Yet, through the work I've done over the many years to tune into my inner guide and my inner "knowing," I hold true that the decision to forge a new partnership with my soon-to-be ex is the right one. The Pause Points and Reflection Questions in this book are intentional and crafted carefully to help you get closer to *your* truth. And if you do the work, it will get easier. These are some of the same questions I have and continue to ask myself.

It's also true that I've had to massively revamp what self-care looks like for me. Given all that's going on in my life currently, and knowing that my value of being a present and engaged parent is still true (and more important than ever before), I have taken self-care to the next level. I engage in and even double up on activities that fuel me on a daily basis, such as meditation and getting out for some exercise, no matter what. These have become nonnegotiables to my sanity. I also make sure that I check in with my community of friends and family to maintain that sense of connection that we all so need (and crave!) during this time. It's become routine for me to look back at the five realms of self-care on a regular basis to check in with myself. I intentionally ask myself, "What do I need now?" so I can continue to fuel myself and my kids to keep moving forward.

That's my journey so far. And you're on your own as we speak. To help you along the way, you can find additional Mommytracked resources at https://soheejunphd.com/resources/. For now, here's what I hope you take away: you *can* forge your own, unique path and create alignment in your life that will give you energy and light you up...in this season and into the next! You can ask for what you want. If you don't get it, ask again. But most of all, keep moving forward with intentional actions that will help you get closer to your unique vision of the mommytrack life.

And I'm here if you need me, the coach in your pocket.

Acknowledgments

You know how they say it takes a village to raise kids? Well, that applies to writing a book as well. And without the support of my "book village," this would never have come to fruition. You know who you are...my amazing supportive tribe of people who cheered me on and gave me valuable feedback when I needed it. Thank you for helping me make this book better than it could've ever been on my own!

To my kids, who inspire me to take risks and to think outside of the box. Tyler, who helped me finalize my book cover. Emma, who is the person I wanted to be at nine. And to Noah, who can always make me laugh!

No matter the challenges I face, there is so much more good because of the people in my life. I'm so thankful for each and every one of you.